TAMBOUR BEAD]
BEGINNERS

A detailed guide to learn the creative art of Indian embroidery and create awesome tambour embroidery patterns from home with great ease

Joan Gabriel

Table of contents

The hummingbird embroidery

CHAPTER ONE

Introduction to Tambour beading

The French embroidery method known as tambour beading involves the use of a hook to produce stitches and adorn textiles with beads and sequins. This technique dates back to the 18th century. This method has been used for decades and has been used to embellish haute couture clothes and accessories. It is still a popular method used in both current fashion and art. In this overview, we will discuss the background of tambour beading as well as its relevance, as well as the instruments and supplies that are required to begin started. In addition, we will go through the several methods and patterns that are involved in tambour beading and provide pointers and advice to assist novices become successful in the endeavor. You will have a thorough comprehension of the art of tambour beading by the time you have finished reading this blueprint, and you will be prepared to give it a try on your own.

The kind of embroidery known as tambour beading requires the use of a particular hook known as a tambour hook in order to create the necessary stitches. Beads, sequins, and many other embellishments, such as rhinestones, are often used using this method for embellishing textiles. The thread is first pushed through the cloth to make a loop, and then the hook is used to capture the thread and hold it. After that, you will need to slide the needle through the loop to make a stitch. Repeating this technique results in more elaborate designs and patterns being created.

Because it gives materials a three-dimensional texture and a sparkling appearance, tambour beading is often employed in haute couture and other forms of high-end fashion. It is also used in the production of costumes for the stage and dance performances. Beading in the tambour style may be carried out on a wide range of materials, such as silk, tulle, velvet, and even leather. The outcomes may be spectacular and one of a kind, but achieving them demands time, expertise, and careful attention to detail.

History of Tambour Beading

The art of tambour beading has its roots in France and dates ack to the 18th century, when it was utilized as a method to adorn expensive textiles for usage by royalty and nobility. The name "tambour" literally translates to "drum" in French, and it is used to describe the frame that resembled a drum and was used to stretch the cloth while it was being worked on. The method rose to prominence during the reign of Louis XV and saw widespread use in haute couture during the 19th and early 20th centuries.

In the beginning, tambour beading was done by hand with the use of a little hook. However, at the end of the 19th century, a new instrument known as the tambour needle was developed.

Because using this tool made the beading process easier, quicker, and more effective, it quickly became the technique of choice for beading tambours. The method remained in demand for the whole of the 20th century and was put to use by illustrious names in the fashion industry such as Chanel, Dior, and Schiaparelli.

Beading in the style of tambour is being utilized in high fashion today, in addition to being employed in modern art and craft. In recent years, there has been an increase in interest in traditional embroidery methods, which has led to a rekindled enthusiasm for the art of tambour beading.

Importance of Tambour Beading

The embroidery method known as tambour beading has been used for centuries and continues to have a place of importance in modern times as well. Throughout history, tambour beading has been an essential element of haute couture and luxury design. It has also been used to embellish clothing and accessories worn by royalty and other members of the upper-class. It was a sign that one belonged to a privileged, sophisticated, and exclusive group.

Tambour beading is still employed in high fashion and couture today, but it has also found a new audience in modern art and craft, particularly in the latter. Tambour beading is one of the classic embroidery methods that is gaining popularity as contemporary designers and artists rediscover its allure and depth of detail. The method enables a diverse array of creative expressions, ranging from basic geometric patterns to intricate, multi-layered graphic compositions.

Beadwork with tambour is prized not just for its attractive appearance but also for its long-lasting quality. Because the method produces a robust and firm adhesive between the beads and the fabric, it is well suited for use in the construction of clothes and accessories that are intended to be used regularly.

In general, the value of tambour beadwork rests in its capacity to produce works of art that are both beautiful and durable, as well as in the cultural and historical relevance it has in the field of needlework and the world of fashion.

CHAPTER THREE

Tools and Materials

In order to get started with tambour beading, there are a few equipment and supplies that you will need. The following is a list of the essential items that you will require:

1. This is the specific hook that is used to generate the stitches, and it is called a tambour hook. It has the appearance of a crochet hook, but the end of it is sharpened into a point, which gives it the ability to puncture cloth.

2. Fabric For tambour beading, you may choose to work with a wide range of textiles, including silk, tulle, velvet, and leather, among others. Choose a fabric that is suitable for the project you are working on and can withstand

the weight of the beads and sequins you will be using.

3. Beads and sequins are the two types of embellishments that will be used to adorn the cloth that you will be working with. To achieve the look you want for your design, you have a broad range of options available to you in terms of color, shape, and size.

4. Thread: You will need a robust and long-lasting thread that is capable of withstanding the weight of the beads and sequins that you will be using. When it comes to tambour beading, many people choose to use Nymo or Fireline.

5. An embroidery hoop is not required, but it is recommended. This will help

you keep the cloth tight as you work on the embroidery.

6. Scissors: In order to cut the thread and trim away any extra fabric, you are going to need a pair of scissors that are very sharp.

7. A design template is not required, but it may be beneficial when developing a pattern and making sure that your beading is consistently spaced and symmetrical. Although this is optional, it can be found here.

You will be able to start designing your very own stunning tambour bead patterns as soon as you have these fundamental equipment and supplies on hand.

Tambour beading stitches

The art of tambour beading incorporates a variety of different methods. The following are some of the needlework methods that are used most often in this style:

1. The chain stitch is the most fundamental technique used in the art of tambour beading. You will first make a loop on the cloth with the tambour hook in order to produce a chain stitch, and then you will feed the needle through the loop in order to secure the stitch. This pattern is often used as the foundation stitch for designs that are more intricate.

2. The bead stitch is a kind of embroidery stitch that involves sewing individual beads onto the cloth. In order to make a bead stitch, first you

will need to thread a bead onto the thread, and then you will need to use the tambour hook to pull the thread, along with the bead, through the cloth. Utilizing this stitch, one may make a wide number of different motifs and patterns.

3. Sequin stitch: The sequin stitch is quite similar to the bead stitch in that it includes connecting individual sequins to the cloth. In order to make this stitch, first you will need to thread a sequin onto the thread, and then you will need to use the tambour hook to pull the thread and the sequin through the cloth. This stitch is used quite often in the process of embellishing a design with shimmer and substance.

4. The look of a fringe or tassel may be achieved by using a stitch known as the fringe stitch. In order to make this stitch, first you will connect a cluster of beads or sequins to the thread, and then, with the tambour hook, you will move the thread along with the beads or sequins in a straight line through the cloth. This stitch may be used to produce a number of different ornamental effects, such as an edge or a trim, depending on how it is worked.

5. A pre-made form or pattern may be attached to the cloth with this stitch, which is called an applique stitch. In order to make this stitch, you will first run the thread through the pre-made form using the tambour hook, and then you will connect the pre-made shape to the cloth. A pattern may be given more

depth and intrigue by using this stitch in the appropriate places.

The art of tambour beading incorporates a wide variety of methods, some of which are included below. You may make a broad range of one-of-a-kind and stunning patterns by combining these methods and experimenting with a variety of beads, sequins, and fabrics.

Stretching the fabric

Beading a tambour requires many steps, one of which is stretching the fabric before beginning. Stretching the fabric before beginning the beading process helps to maintain the fabric's tautness and prevents it from becoming wrinkled or misshapen when the beads are applied. The following are some suggestions for how to stretch the fabric:

1. Utilize an embroidery hoop: an embroidery hoop is a circular frame that keeps the cloth in a tight position while you embroider on it. After the fabric has been positioned within the hoop, the screws should be tightened until the cloth is stretched to its full length. In order to avoid any puckering, you must first ensure that the cloth is spread uniformly inside the hoop.

2. Utilize a stretcher frame: A stretcher frame is like to an embroidery hoop; however, it has clamps that are adjustable and may be tightened in order to stretch the cloth to its full length. When working with bigger

amounts of fabric or with materials that are difficult to hoop, this is a wonderful alternative to consider.

3. T-pin the fabric to a board: If you do not have an embroidery hoop or a stretcher frame, you may use T-pins to attach the cloth to a board or another flat surface. Before pinning the cloth in place, make sure that it is stretched out evenly and to a tight state.

4. Utilize a fabric stretcher A fabric stretcher is a specialized piece of equipment that may be utilized in order to stretch a piece of cloth to its maximum potential. It is constructed out of wood and has clamps that can be adjusted to varying degrees in order to get the desired degree of cloth stretching. When working with bigger

amounts of fabric or with materials that are difficult to hoop, this is a wonderful alternative to consider.

After the cloth has been stretched, you can then begin the process of beading the tambour. Be careful to check the tension of the fabric at regular intervals during the beading process and make any necessary adjustments to avoid the cloth from becoming misshapen or puckered.

Threading the tambour hook

The method of making a tambourine begins with the threading of the tambour hook, which is an essential step. This is the procedure to follow:

1. Choose your thread: When choosing your thread, be sure to choose one that is suitable for the project you are

working on. When it comes to tambour beading, prominent alternatives include Nymo and Fireline.

2. Your thread has to be cut: Cut a piece of thread that is long enough to finish the beading pattern you want to make, plus a little bit more so that you have room to tie knots and secure the thread.

3. The first step in threading the needle is to pass the free end of the thread through the eye of the tambour hook. A needle threader might be helpful in situations when the thread is too thick to pass through the eye of the needle.

4. Make a knot: At the very end of the thread, make a knot to prevent it from coming undone and falling out of the hook.

5. Hold the hook: To hold the hook, place your thumb and forefinger on the center of the shaft of the tambourine, similar to how you would hold a pencil.

6. To pierce the fabric, place the point of the hook on the underside of the cloth in the location where you wish to begin your beading project. This will allow you to puncture the fabric. When you push the hook through the cloth, you should take care to penetrate only one of the fabric layers at a time.

7. After the hook has penetrated the cloth, you should drag it through to the correct side of the fabric by using the 'pull the hook through' command. It is important that the thread follows the hook and is pulled through the cloth at the same time.

8. Repeat: Carry out this procedure several times in order to construct a chain stitch base for your beadwork design.

If you follow these instructions, you will have no trouble threading the tambour hook and getting started on your beading project with a tambour. Make sure that you practice your technique on a piece of scrap fabric before beginning your actual project, and always check the tension of your threads to make sure that they are equal and constant.

Starting and ending the thread
It is crucial to begin and terminate the thread in the correct manner for your tambour beading project to guarantee that the finished product is tidy and

professional looking. The following are some suggestions for beginning and concluding your post:

To begin the conversation:

1. Knot the thread: At the very end of your thread, tie a knot, being sure to leave a tail that is sufficiently long to be woven in later.

2. To prevent the thread from unraveling, begin by piercing the fabric with the hook at the spot where you want the pattern to begin, and then draw the thread through to the correct side of the cloth.

3. Make the foundation chain: To make the foundation chain for your beading design, you may use the chain stitch method.

4. After you have finished the foundation chain, you will need to weave the tail of the thread back through the stitches to hold it in place. You may do this by pulling it through the backwards.

To wrap up this line of thought:

1. Weave in the tail: Once you have completed the beading pattern you were working on, pull the tail of the thread through the stitches on the wrong side of the cloth and weave it in.

2. Knot the thread: To keep the tail from sliding out of position, tie a knot at the end of the tail.

3. Reduce the length of the thread by cutting it as near as possible to the knot.

4. Conceal the knot: If you want to, you may use a needle to draw the knot into the cloth so that it is entirely concealed. This is an option.

If you follow these instructions, you will be able to finish your tambour beading project such that it appears clean and organized, without any obvious knots or loose threads. Always remember to check the tension of your stitches to verify that they are equal and constant before beginning your final product, and practice your starting and finishing methods on spare fabric before beginning your actual project.

Beading and sequin placement

When it comes to the beading and the positioning of the sequins in the tambour beading, there are a few essential elements to bear in mind in order to obtain a tidy and expert-looking finish. Here are some tips:

1. Before beginning work on your tambour beading project, it is important to first sketch out your design on paper or use a computer program to do it. This will make it easier for you to imagine how you want your beads and sequins to be arranged on the cloth, and it will also help you guarantee that the spacing between the beads and sequins is constant and balanced.

2. Be careful to use beads and sequins that are the appropriate size and form for your design. This will help ensure that your creation turns out just as you envisioned it. Beads and sequins of various sizes may be utilized to create

pieces that make a powerful statement, while tiny beads and sequins can be used to create more delicate patterns.

3. Be consistent with the spacing and positioning of your beads and sequins: To ensure that your design seems tidy and professional, it is important to be consistent with the spacing and placement of your beads and sequins as you are putting them. Make certain that there is an equal spacing between each bead or sequin by using a ruler or a measuring tape to do so.

4. Utilize the Appropriate Equipment It is essential to make use of the appropriate equipment in order to achieve a finish that is both clean and accurate. When cutting the thread, you should be sure to use a pair of sharp

scissors, and when weaving in the ends, you should use a very thin needle. Tweezers are another tool that might come in handy when picking up and positioning little beads and sequins.

5. Beads and sequins should be secured by using a little dot of glue or a knot at the end of each thread. This will guarantee that your beads and sequins do not fall off while you are working. In the long run, this will prevent them from moving or slipping off.

You can create a tambour beading project that looks elegant and professional if you practice your technique and follow these suggestions. The project will have beads and sequins that are arranged in an orderly fashion.

Patterns

Tambour beading enables the creation of an almost infinite variety of different patterns and styles. The following are some examples of popular patterns:

1. patterns based on flowers and other types of botanicals are common choices for tambour beadwork. This is because to the ease with which the delicate forms and intricacies of these patterns can be created with the use of the tambour hook.

2. Designs based on geometry: Diamonds, triangles, and squares are some of the most common types of geometric patterns used in tambour beading. Beads and sequins may be used in conjunction with one another to produce these patterns, which will

result in a polished, contemporary appearance.

3. Abstract patterns and motifs may also be created with the help of tambour beading, which is an excellent medium for such projects. You may create one-of-a-kind designs that stand out by playing around with a variety of elements, including colors, forms, and textures.

4. Patterns of animals: The tambour beading technique may also be used to make patterns of animals, such as birds, butterflies, and other types of creatures. Beads and sequins may be used in conjunction with one another to provide the rough and layered appearance desired for these designs.

5. Designs for bridal and formal wear: The tambour beading technique is often used in the embellishment of bridal and formal wear, such as on wedding gowns, evening dresses, and ball gowns. These designs often make use of complex beading and sequin work in order to provide a dazzling and sophisticated appearance.

When it comes to the creation of patterns and designs with tambour beads, the possibilities are almost limitless, regardless of your level of skill as a tambour beader. You only need a little ingenuity and some experience to come up with stunning and one-of-a-kind patterns that highlight your abilities and sense of fashion.

CHAPTER THREE

Basic tambour beading patterns

There are a few fundamental designs for tambour beading that are simple to pick up and are an excellent choice for novices. To get you started, here are three different patterns:

1. Stitching a Straight Line The straight stitch is one of the most fundamental stitches used in tambour beading. To make a straight stitch, you will need to thread a bead onto your tambour hook and then enter the hook from the reverse side of the cloth. To construct the next stitch, you will need to first draw the hook through to the front of the cloth and then re-insert it into the fabric a little distance away. Proceed

with the stitching in this manner to make a beaded line that is straight.

2. The chain stitch is another fundamental tambour beading technique that is straightforward to master. Beads should be threaded onto the tambour hook, and then the hook should be inserted into the cloth from the reverse side to produce a chain stitch. After bringing the hook to the front of the work, you will need to re-introduce it into the cloth at the beginning of the first stitch. After pulling the hook through the cloth to form a loop, you will need to re-insert it into the material a little distance away in order to produce the next stitch. Carry on sewing in this manner so that you end up with a chain of loops.

3. Beaded fringe: Beaded fringe is a basic tambour beading pattern that may be used to give texture and movement to a design. Beaded fringe can be created by stringing beads in a fringe pattern. To produce beaded fringe, first string numerous beads onto your tambour hook, then put the hook into the cloth from the reverse side. After you have pulled the hook through to the front, you should then re-hook it into the material a short distance away. Continue doing so in order to produce a string of beaded fringe. You may create a diverse and attractive design by varying the length of each fringe as well as the quantity of beads used in each fringe.

You will be able to construct a wide range of motifs and patterns if you are able to master these fundamental tambour beading patterns. As your familiarity with the method increases, you will be able to explore with a wider variety of stitches, beads, and sequins, which will allow you to create patterns that are more complicated and elaborate.

Straight stitch

The straight stitch is a fundamental tambour beading stitch that is often used for the purpose of producing lines of beads or sequins that are perfectly straight. This is the procedure to follow:

1. Beads or sequins may be threaded through your tambour hook.

2. At the spot in the cloth where you will begin stitching, insert the hook into

the back of the fabric so that it faces the front.

3. You may either bring the bead or the sequin with you when you pull the hook through to the front of the cloth.

4. After moving the hook a little distance away from the previous hole in the cloth, insert it again into the fabric and then draw it through to the rear of the fabric.

5. Repeat steps 2–4 in order to make a line of beads or sequins that is straight.

6. Make a knot at the back of the cloth to hold the end of the thread, and cut off any extra thread when the knot is complete.

It is essential that the tension on the thread be maintained at the same level throughout the creation of straight stitches. If the tension is not tight enough, the beads or sequins may slide down the cloth or perhaps fall off entirely. It's possible that the cloth may pucker or stretch if the tension is too high. Before beginning your project, it is recommended that you first practice adjusting the tension on a scrap piece of cloth.

Chain stitch

The chain stitch is yet another fundamental tambour beading stitch that may be used to produce a wide range of different motifs and patterns. This is the procedure to follow:

1. Beads or sequins may be threaded through your tambour hook.

2. At the spot in the cloth where you will begin stitching, insert the hook into the back of the fabric so that it faces the front.

3. You may either bring the bead or the sequin with you when you pull the hook through to the front of the cloth.

4. Place the hook back into the cloth at the beginning of the first stitch, but this time, instead of dragging the thread through to the back of the fabric, leave a loop of it on the front of the fabric.

5. Bring the hook back up through the loop on the front side of the cloth, then bring the hook back down through the fabric.

6. Insert the hook back into the cloth a little distance away from the original

stitch, and then thread another bead or sequin onto the hook.

7. Repeat steps 4-6 in order to construct a chain of stitches by drawing the hook through the back of the cloth and bringing it to the front.

8. Make a knot at the back of the cloth to hold the end of the thread, and cut off any extra thread when the knot is complete.

It is possible to make curving lines using the chain stitch, in addition to more complicated motifs like flowers and leaves. You may make a chain stitch that is either more or less snug by adjusting the tension on the thread you are using. Before beginning your project, it is recommended that you get the feel of the process by first practicing on an old scrap of cloth.

Beaded fringe

Beaded fringe is a simple method for creating tambour beadwork that may be used to give a design more texture and motion. This is the procedure to follow:

1. Beads or sequins should be threaded onto the hook used for the tambourine.

2. At the place where you want to begin attaching your fringe, work the hook through the back of the cloth and out the front.

3. You may draw the beads or sequins through to the front of the cloth by pulling the hook through to the front.

4. Place the hook back into the cloth a little distance away from the initial stitch. However, rather of drawing the thread completely through to the back of the fabric, leave a loop of thread on the front side of the fabric.

5. After adding more beads or sequins to the hook, re-peg the hook into the cloth by passing it through the loop located on the front of the piece.

6. Repeat steps 2-5 in order to produce a line of beaded fringe on the cloth by first pulling the hook through to the reverse side of the fabric.

7. Insert the hook through the cloth from the back to the front, adjacent to the stitch that was just completed. This will complete the fringe.

8. To make the fringe more secure, pull the hook through the back of the cloth until it reaches the front, and then tie a knot in the thread.

Beaded fringe may be used to adorn the edges of garments or accessories, or it can be used to create texture and movement to a larger design. Both of these functions can be accomplished by using beaded fringe. Adjusting the amount of beads or sequins on your hook as well as the distance between each stitch will allow you to make the fringe either longer or shorter. Before beginning your project, it is recommended that you first perfect the method by working on a piece of cloth scrap.

Maintaining tension

When practicing tambour beading, it is essential to keep the tension even throughout the process in order to obtain clean and uniform stitches. The following are some suggestions on how to keep the tension up:

1. While you work on the project, you may keep the cloth tight by using a frame or a hoop. Stitching in this manner won't cause the cloth to pucker or stretch out as much as it would otherwise.

2. The cloth should be held in the hand that is not your dominant hand, while the tambour hook and thread should be used with the one that is your dominant hand.

3. While you stitch, you may keep the thread tight by pulling it ever-so-

slightly with your thumb and fingers as you stitch. Because of this, the beads or sequins won't get loose or slide off as easily.

4. As you stitch, make sure you pay attention to the tension. Before moving on with the project, readjust the tension if you see that the thread is becoming more loose or that the cloth is beginning to pucker.

5. Before beginning your project, it is recommended that you first practice adjusting the tension on a scrap piece of cloth.

Throughout the process of tambour beading, if you maintain tension, you will be able to make stitches that are both clean and uniform, which will contribute to the enhancement of your design.

CHAPTER FOUR

Choosing the right fabric

When creating tambour beading, selecting the appropriate fabric is essential since it has an impact on the level of difficulty associated with stitching, the overall beauty of the final design, and the longevity of the decoration. The following are some pointers to consider while selecting the appropriate fabric for your project including tambour beading:

1. Choose a fabric that has a dense weave and can withstand the weight of the beads or sequins you want to use. Stay away from materials that are very thin or elastic since they are more likely to distort or warp as you sew on them.

2. Choose a fabric that will not snag or catch on the tambour hook by going with one that has a smooth surface. Silk, cotton, and wool are all excellent alternatives when it comes to fabrics.

3. Think about how the hue and pattern of the cloth will work with the design you have in mind. It's possible that a fabric with a solid color may highlight the ornamentation more successfully than one with a pattern, while a fabric with a textured pattern will add to the visual intrigue of the design.

4. Consider the final purpose that will be served by the completed product. Choose a robust fabric that will endure wear and tear if you are going to be designing an item of clothing or an

accessory that will be worn regularly or handled frequently.

5. Before beginning the project, you should do a few test stitches on the cloth to evaluate its quality. This will provide you with a better understanding of how the fabric behaves and whether or not it is appropriate for your requirements.

You can guarantee that the pattern you create with tambour beading turns out beautifully and will hold up well over the course of many years if you use the appropriate fabric.

Choosing the appropriate needle size to use

When creating tambour beading, choosing the appropriate needle size is essential since it has an effect on both the degree of difficulty and the size of the stitch produced. Here are some pointers to consider when selecting the appropriate needle size for your project with tambour beads:

1. Select a needle that has a diameter that corresponds with the size of the bead or sequin that you will be working with. When working with bigger beads or sequins, you'll need a larger needle, whereas working with tiny beads or sequins calls for a smaller needle.

2. Take into account the thickness of the thread that you are using. If the thread is really fine, you may require a needle that is a size or two smaller in order to create a secure stitch.

3. Consider the kind of material you're dealing with in terms of the fabric. In

order to prevent causing damage to the fabric, you may want to use a smaller needle if it is very fragile.

4. Before beginning the craft, you need do a few test stitches to determine the correct needle size. This will give you an idea of how the size of the needle influences the size of the stitch as well as the ease with which it may be stitched.

5. If you are unsure of the needle size to use, begin with a needle that is of a medium size and change the size as necessary depending on your expertise.

If you choose the appropriate needle size for the tambour beading project you are working on, you will be able to guarantee that your stitches are secure and that the pattern you create will turn out beautifully.

Troubleshooting common problems
Tambour beading, like any other kind of beadwork, may come with its fair share of difficulties. The following is a list of frequent issues that may arise when you are working with tambour beads, as well as some suggestions for resolving these issues:

1. Beads or sequins are coming loose; this might be because there is not enough tension on the thread, or it could be because you are using a needle that is too little in comparison to the size of the bead or sequin. Adjusting the tension on the thread, using a bigger needle, or attempting to

use a stronger thread are all potential solutions to this problem.

2. The stitches are not even: If the tension on the thread is not constant or if you do not maintain the cloth tight while you stitch, this may be the reason of the uneven stitches. To resolve this issue, you should make an effort to retain a constant tension on the thread and make use of a frame or hoop to keep the cloth tight.

3. If you are using a thread that is too long or if you are not keeping the thread tight while you stitch, this may be the reason of the thread becoming tangled. Make use of shorter lengths of thread and pull the thread tight during stitching in order to correct this issue.

4. The problem might be that you are not using a needle that is sharp enough, or that you are using a needle that is too big in comparison to the size of the bead or sequin you are working with. If you want to remedy this problem, consider using a needle that is either smaller or sharper.

5. The puckering of the cloth may have been produced by either pushing the thread through the fabric at too great of a tension or by using a needle that was too big for the fabric. To solve this, adjust the tension on the thread, and then use a needle that is one size smaller than you normally would.

You'll be able to conquer the hurdles of tambour beading and produce patterns of stunning beauty and superior quality if you learn how to solve these typical issues first.

CHAPTER FIVE

Step by step Tambour Embroidery guide

What is needed for tambour embroidery?

The tambourine needle is a specialized kind of crochet needle that is very tiny and pointed. Be sure that the aperture of the needle is facing in the same direction as the locking screw before you attempt to insert the needle. During the stitching process, it is much simpler to determine in which direction the crochet points because of this. Beginners in tambour should begin by practicing on a scrap of cloth, during which they should experiment with a variety of stitching and textile embellishment methods. Tulle is another option, however organza is the most ideal choice for this use. If you have a good feel for how to use the needle, you should be able to translate this sort of embroidery to other types of fabrics as well. Threads that are appropriate include things like "Fil a Gant," silk thread, embroidery twist, and metallic thread, among others. It is advised that you practice the fundamental chain stitch in a variety of sizes as a means of getting started. After that, you may experiment with surface embroidery, embroidery in a circle, and gorgeous corner embroidery. Finally, beads or sequins are another option for embellishment that may be used. Because the embroidery hoop does not need to be handled, a specialized embroidery hoop may be used to embroider the tambourine, which allows the user to have both hands free.

How to secure when you start the bead

To begin, we will demonstrate how the problem at the seam's commencement may be rectified. In order to provide a clearer demonstration, the stitch is worked a little bit bigger than is strictly required. If you want to avoid drawing any attention to the stitches that are used for attaching anything, you should make them as little as possible.

1 Take the embroidery thread and encircle it around your pointer finger, securing it in place with your thumb on your second finger. Hold it underneath the embroidery frame. This will produce tension in the thread.

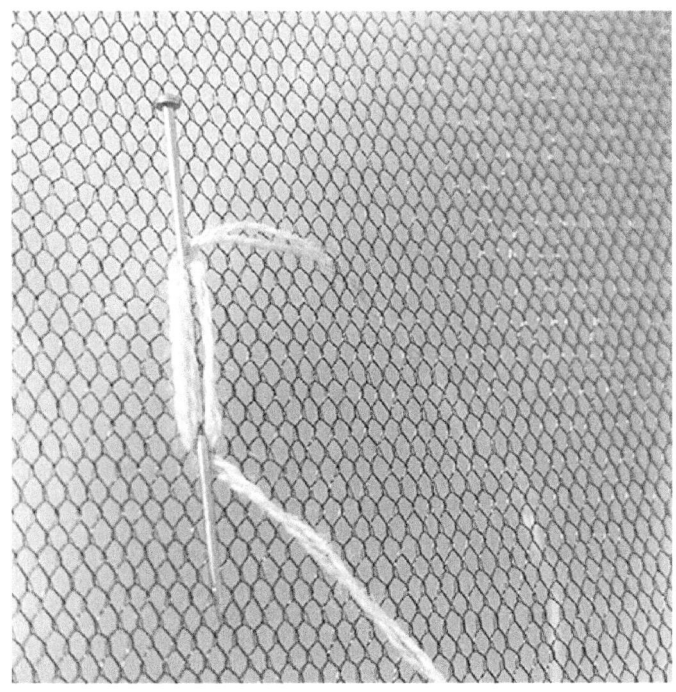

2 Prick the beginning of the yarn with the tambourine needle from above, and then pull the beginning of the yarn up. Put the needle on the edge of the yarn, and then, in order to secure it, wrap the beginning of the yarn around the needle three times.

3 The needle is inserted from above for the first stitch, and it is done so some distance away from the beginning of the thread. Both the aperture in the needle and the screw that secures it should always point in the direction of the embroidery being done, which is to the right in this example. It is important to keep the needle held as

vertically as possible during the process of sewing in order to prevent the thread from becoming tangled.

4 Next, wrap the yarn around the needle from behind once, completing one full revolution, and then flip the needle around 180 degrees clockwise so that the opening and the screw are

facing left. Pulling the yarn ever-so-slightly with your fingers can help you achieve a higher tension and keep the yarn from slipping through the needle hook. Now that we've reached this point, we can bring the thread to the surface. Now that the last stitch is complete, the thread tension may be relaxed once again in order to make ready for the following one.

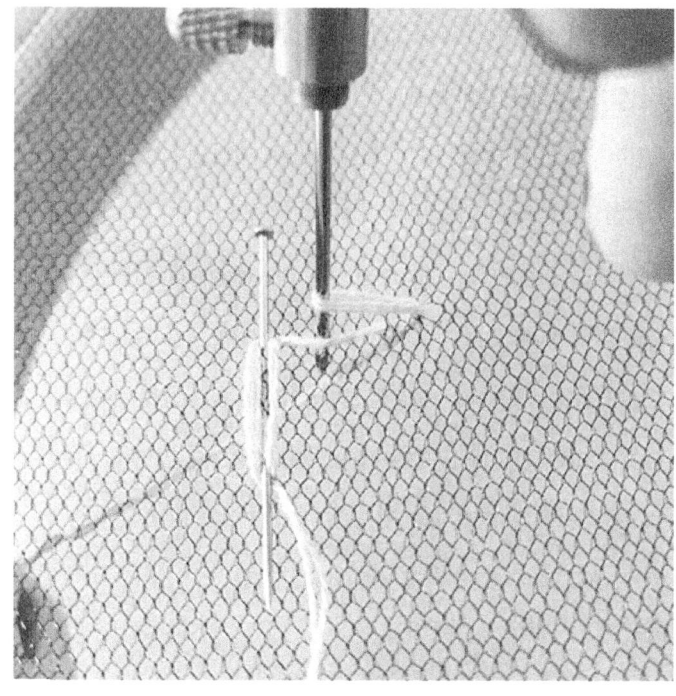

5 The needle is already in the right position for a reverse stitch, which should finish behind the first thread. This stitch should be completed behind the first stitch.

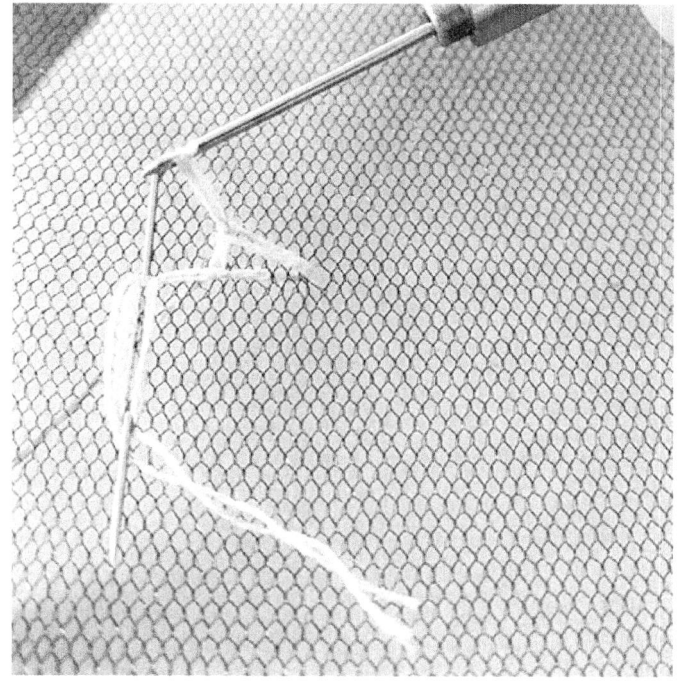

6 After you have completed the reverse stitch, coil the thread around the needle once more, spin the needle around 180 degrees, secure the thread in the hook, and draw it to the surface. The loop should run through the stitch that was just completed.

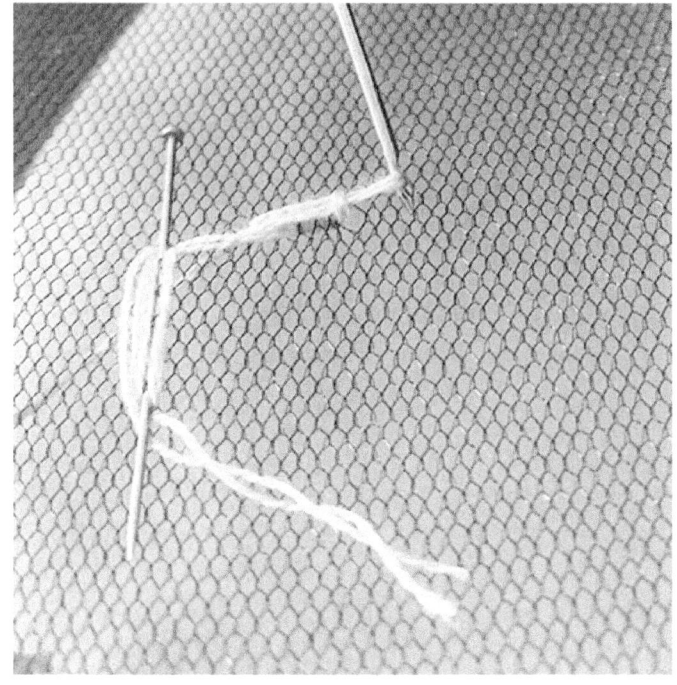

7 When the new loop is moved to the right, the preceding loop travels along with it and continues to move with it. Now you need to draw the thread through the embroidery hoop from the bottom up so that you may tighten the previous loop.

8 The very last of the three safety
stitches may be found just after the
very first stitch. After inserting the
needle, the yarn is now wrapped
around the crochet a second time; after
that, the crochet is rotated through 180
degrees and the loop is pulled up.

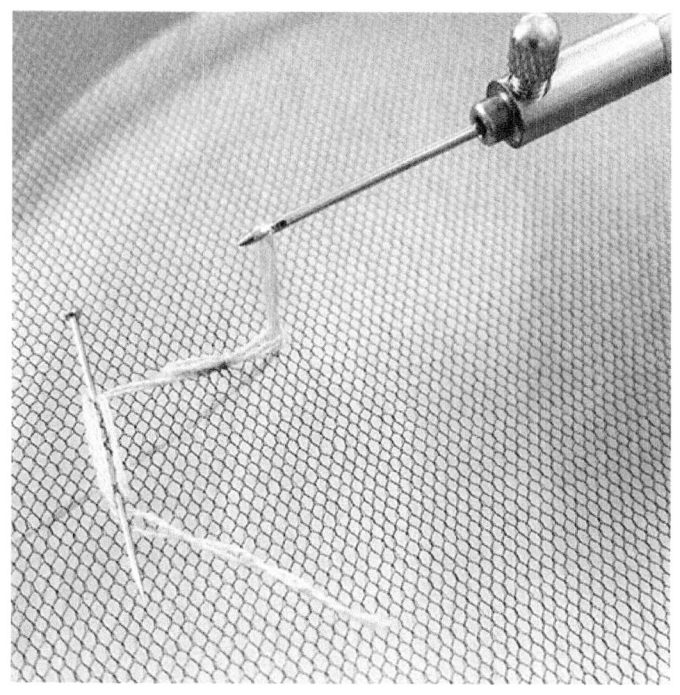

9 When you have completed these three processes, which are the insertion, the back stitch, and the forward stitch, the seam will be fixed, and you may then begin the embroidery itself.

Chain Stitch

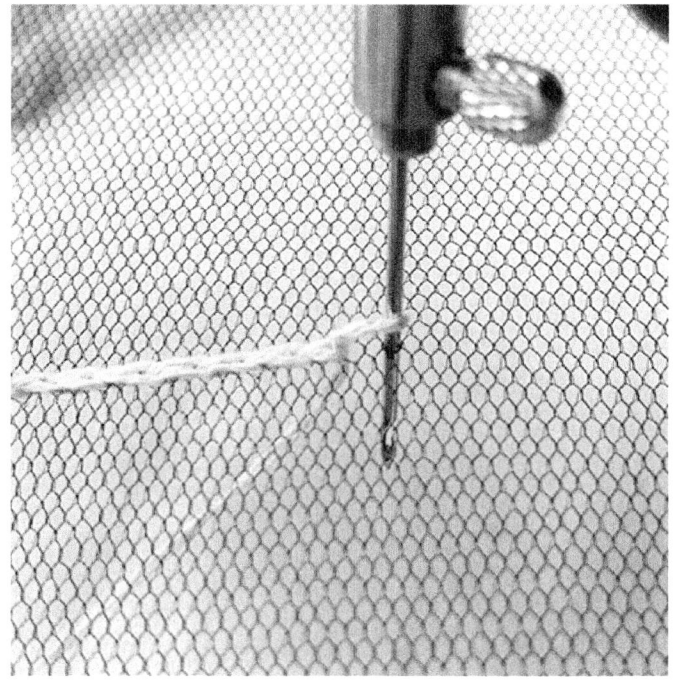

The chain stitch may be used to create straight lines or to fill up larger spaces completely. The basic idea is the same as it is for the stitch used to secure anything, with the exception that all stitches are worked forward here.

CHAPTER SIX

Bead embroidery design

If you have ever seen a fashion show for haute couture, you have probably seen the magnificent embroidery patterns that blend thread, sequins, and beads to create amazing intricate designs that embellish evening dresses, collars, or possibly jacket cuffs. These designs can be found decorating evening gowns, collars, or jacket cuffs. Handwork is essential to the production of elaborate patterns used in haute couture. There are instances in which whole skirts are covered with beautiful swirls made of beads and thread. How are such things created?

Tambour embroidery is often the correct response.

A tambour hook, which is very similar in appearance to a pointed crochet hook, is used to create tambour embroidery. You can crochet right through the cloth if you have a hook, and the pace of your work will go up significantly. Long rows of beads may be created by threading beads and sequins onto the yarn and including them between the "hookings" in the pattern.

You'll need to work on the cloth from both the front and the back. One hand is used to drive the tambour hook through the cloth from the other side, while the other hand is used to wrap the thread around it on the opposite side of the fabric. When the thread is twisted around, the hook will capture it, and then the thread will be drawn through the cloth as well as the stitch that came before it. The real design is generated on the "wrong side" of the cloth, which is particularly important to keep in mind while working with beads. Because of this, it is helpful to use a transparent fabric as a basis, such as silk organza. This will allow you to readily see what you are doing as you work.

Materials and supplies needed

The following is a brief list of the items that I used in my work:

• tambour hook

- silk organza

- a frame (I made mine out of pieces of an old frame that held a silk picture.)

- a stapler in addition to staples

- cotton twill tape, either 3 or 4 centimeters in width

- the thread used for embroidery

- a twist in the buttonhole

- sewing thread made of polyester (the standard kind)

- rhinestones, beads, and sequins

- pins

- Needles, including some very fine ones that are able to pass through the holes in your beads.

You may choose the hook that is most appropriate for the task at hand and then screw it in place.

How to mount the frame

As I indicated before, I used various components of the frame for my silk painting. Inasmuch as I was unable to keep the frame's sides at the same level, it did not function in the most ideal manner; yet, it did its job adequately.

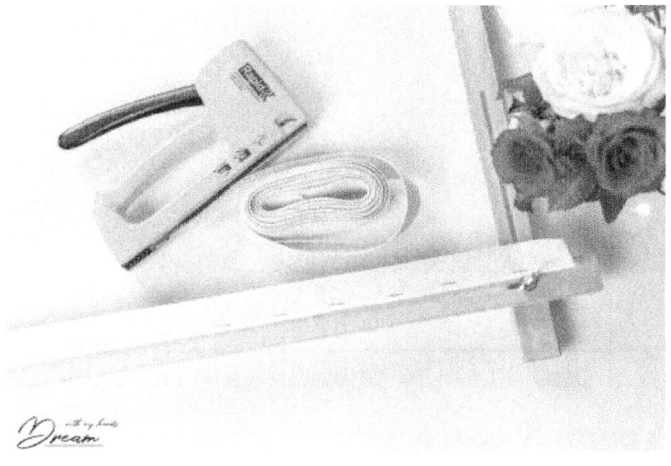

I knew I had some silk organza in my stockpile, so I decided to use a piece of that and cut it into a rectangle. In order to mount my silk to the frame, I first attached twill tape to two sides of the frame that were opposite one another. After that, I was able to attach my silk organza to the twill tape by using the following method:

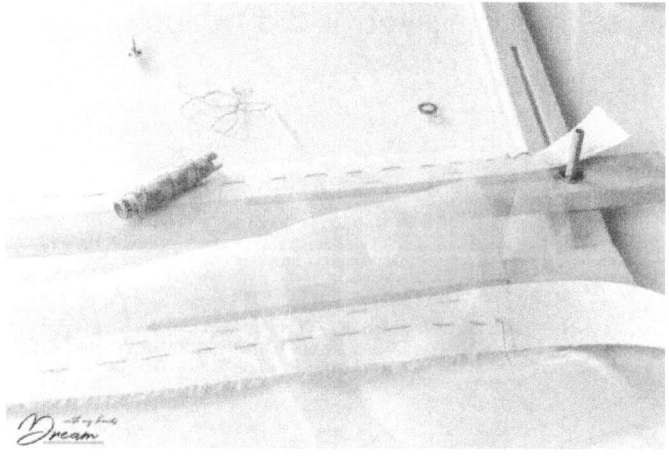

Although I used silk buttonhole twist, you may use whatever sort of thread you choose; nevertheless, it is preferable if the thread is robust. The typical thread for topstitching would perform well in this application.

After that, I pulled the fabric taut over the framework. Pinned to twill tape that was looped around both sides of the frame, the sides were assembled as follows:

Basic tambour stitch

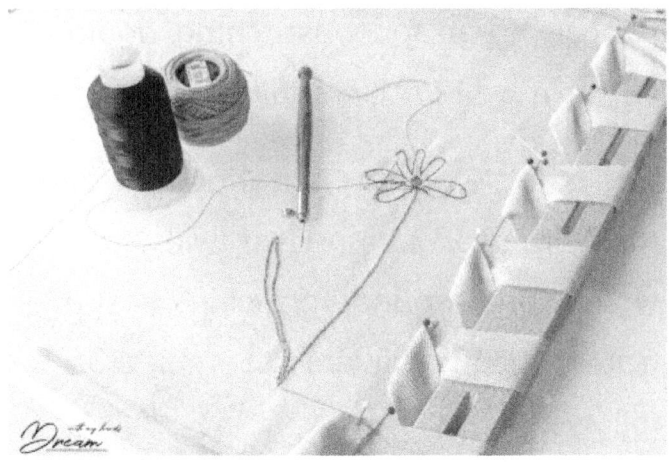

Learning the fundamental stitch and how to work in both an outward and inward direction was the first skill you needed to acquire. When changing directions, I discovered that it is necessary to alter both the direction in which the thread is being wrapped and the direction in which the hook is being turned. To begin, I took some DMC Cotton Perle thread in Gold and used it to make a floral stem and a leaf.

In order to determine the location of the hook, you will need to adjust it so that it is aligned with the screw in the holder. When you pass through the cloth, make sure the hook is pointed in the same direction as you are travelling. After that, you will wind the thread around the hook in an anti-clockwise orientation, going all the way around it. This step is based on the assumption that you are working away from you. After that, rotate the hook through 180 degrees counterclockwise, then draw it back through the cloth while simultaneously expanding the hole with the rear of the hook. This will ensure that the hook passes through the fabric smoothly and will prevent it from snagging. When you reverse course and go in the opposite direction of you, you will wind the thread around the hook while turning it in a counterclockwise manner.

Following that, I experimented with constructing a flower out of Raiman Rayon Machine Embroidery Thread.

I thought that the cotton perle thread gave off an attractive appearance. The machine embroidery thread, on the other hand, was a little bit too frail and thin, and the look it produced was not very pleasing. It's possible that it worked with beads, but even if it did, you could just as easily use regular thread for your sewing machine.

When working with a crochet hook, the chain stitch is created on the side that the hook is working on. The reverse side reveals a continuous line of stitches, as follows:

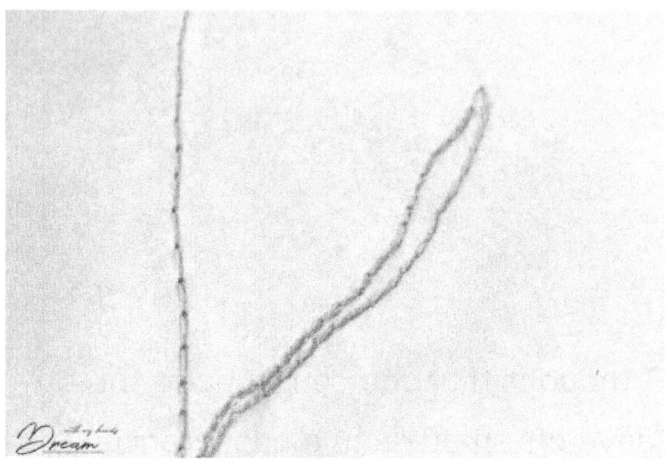

You are free to utilize any side you would like. If you prefer to work from the opposite side, you may also turn the fabric and the frame so that they are facing you.

How to carry out Tambour beading

I have several glass beads in yellow, orange, and red colors with a thickness of 2-3 millimeters. When you first begin the process of tambour beading, all of the beads should already be in the tread. When I was threading the beads onto my thread, I used a very fine needle. I followed the instructions in one of the videos and brought the beginning thread over to the working side, where I then stitched it down a few times to secure it. After that, I got to work constructing the string of beads.

If you are right handed, hold your beads in your left hand. If you are left handed, hold your beads in your right hand. After passing through the cloth, you will use your left hand to position one of the beads, and then you will wind your thread around the hook to secure the position of the bead. After that, you will complete the stitch in the exact same manner as you did while you were working on the fundamental stitch.

From the perspective of the workers, the job seems as follows:

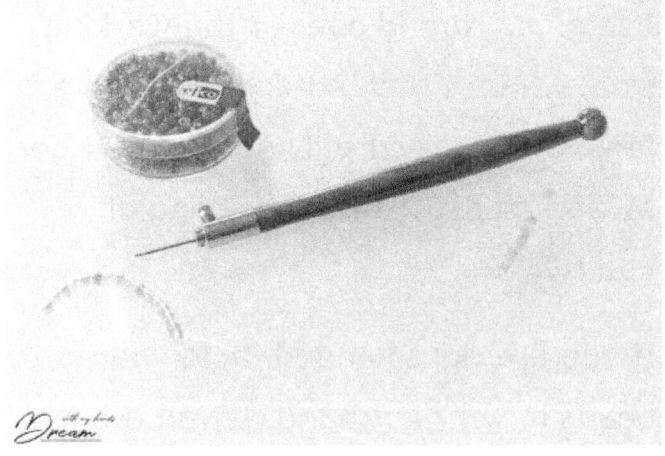

This is the string of beads that is made on the opposite side, often known as the "right" side:

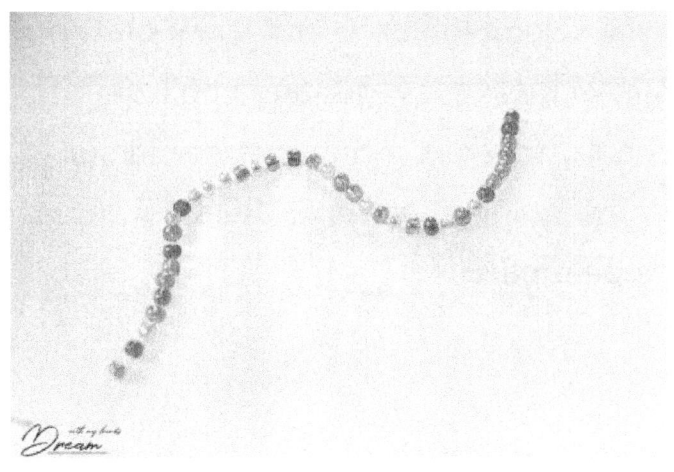

Sequins

Sequins may be thought of as flattened beads. You may arrange them next to each other as I did, or you can overlap them like I did here. When I originally started, I wasn't really sure which direction the beads were supposed to be strung in. In conclusion, I don't believe that it actually makes a difference. It will depend on how you want your needlework to appear as well as how you want to flip the sequins when you ultimately put them on the project. Give it a go, and you'll see what I mean. On the reverse side of the sequins, they have the following appearance:

The hummingbird embroidery

Even after spending a lot of time online, I had a hard time finding a pattern that I liked. After much deliberation, I decided to go with this image of an embroidered hummingbird that I saw online but can no longer locate. In any case, I printed it out at the size I desired, and then I used a marker that could be erased to sketch my pattern directly into the silk. After that, I used my tambour hook to embroider the contour of the object.

Since I had a large supply of beads and sequins in storage, I decided to play with the positioning of the beads and the colors until I reached a point where I was satisfied. Because I was unable to create any longer rows of beads, I made the decision to convert to a different kind of stitching.

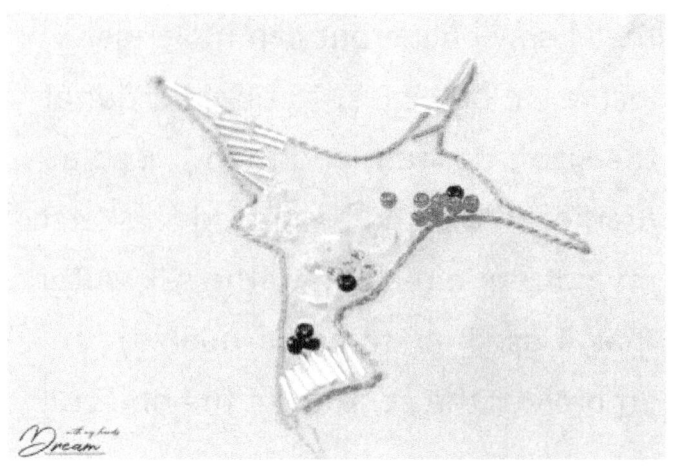

After beginning with the hummingbird's tail, I made my way around the bird, adding extra cotton perle stitches here and there in order to clarify the intricacies and some satin stitches there. I did my best to replicate the color patterns from the original photo, despite the fact that the colors I chose were not at all similar to those in the original and that I used beads in addition to embroidery thread. I have

to say that I am really pleased with
how this little' dude turned out.

Dream

I am considering creating a pair of
identical pieces that are a mirror image
of each other for it so that I may sew
them on as a pair. Following that, I
want to try beading on a tambourine
more by making a little handbag out of
beads.

Increasing one's knowledge is almost
always enjoyable.

I really hope that this little instruction was helpful to you. Collect the necessary materials, then proceed to construct your hummingbird.

Printed in Great Britain
by Amazon

59973317R00057